RECKLESS DESIGN: WILD SURRENDER

RECKLESS DESIGN: WILD SURRENDER

KATIE WELLS

Reckless Design: Wild Surrender
© 2015 by Katie Wells

ISBN: 1514387123
ISBN 13: 9781514387122
Library of Congress Control Number: 2015909869

CreateSpace Independent Publishing Platform
North Charleston, South Carolina
Cover by SaintDisegno
www.saintdisegno.com

CONTENTS

ACKNOWLEDGMENTS

To my only reason for existence: God, my Holy Father and friend. He is truly the author of this story, and to Him I am eternally grateful.

I am forever grateful to my mom for always being my biggest cheerleader; she has put countless hours and resources into helping make this book a reality.

Thank you to my dad for taking me to a Baptist church in Syracuse, New York, when I was six years old. It was there that I gave my life to Christ.

I'm thankful to both of my parents for taking me to LaFayette Christian and Missionary Alliance Church throughout all of my childhood; there I learned about the truths of God while I was in every children's and youth program possible.

For all the families and individuals at LaFayette Alliance Church who invested in me and believed that God was working in and through me, thank you. You are like family to me.

I will always be grateful for Delta Lake Bible Camp in Rome, New York, where I spent part of every summer of my childhood and youth. God mightily used presenters at that camp to speak into my life. It was there, at age eleven, that I heard God's call to take His Word to those who have never heard it.

I am thankful for my professors and the leadership at Northwestern College in St. Paul, Minnesota, where I learned so much about God, people, and ministry.

Many thanks to Hope Community Church in Circle Pines, Minnesota. You took me in as one of your own while I was in college and then supported me when I was commissioned to be an international worker in Bolivia.

South America Mission and the Bolivia international workers were my closest family for eight years while I lived in South America. I love you, friends.

Muchas gracias to my dear Bolivian brothers and sisters who walked with me as we sought God together.

ONE

COME ALONG WITH ME

A small clearing holds the cemetery...a ten-minute walk north of the village, through the forest and brush of eastern Bolivia. There is only one aboveground concrete box with a cross made of metal. The rest of the clearing has simple, weathered wooden crosses near body-shaped mounds of dirt. I had come here before—alone.

This time, nine-year-old Phillip accompanied me. His grandmother, Anna, was my friend. Anna had request-ed that I paint her late husband's name and the dates of his birth and death on the wooden cross that stood over his body. Painting that cross for Anna was a way I could serve her family, showing them I care about them. Phillip helped me, occasionally handing me a tube of oil paint or the gasoline I used for paint thinner. The sun beat down on us that morning, and the mosquitoes continually reminded us that we were in their territory. Some people walked past the cemetery on the dirt road, seeming surprised to see us sitting there. I had the wonderful realization that God had led me to that cemetery to do a task others had never done nor would be willing to do.

While we were sitting in the cemetery, it was impossible to not think about life, death, God, and eternity. I asked Phillip what he thought about those things. He believed the spirits of the dead are still present on the earth. Bolivians have the custom of putting candles on the graves so that the spirits of the deceased can find their way back to their graves. Occasionally family members leave the favorite foods and liquors of their loved ones by the graves to please the spirits that they believe still linger there, as some Bolivians live in fear of the dead.

As we continued to work, I told Phillip that we were painting the cross to remember his grandfather and to honor his grandmother's request, not to please the grandfather's spirit. As I spoke, God laid out the perfect opportunity to explain to Phillip what the Bible teaches about death and where people go after they die. He listened intently despite the uncomfortable conditions and the strange classroom in which we had found ourselves.

Later, we worked on memorizing a Bible verse for the Thursday-night Bible study at his aunt's house. Phillip and Anna came on a regular basis to the family Bible study. Phillip enjoyed memorizing verses and was able to answer questions about the verses and Bible lessons. I do not know if Phillip became a Christian in the cemetery as we painted the old wooden cross under the hot sun. The truth I was telling him from the Bible was radically different from anything he had been told before. Was he able to disregard his entire belief system after a simple conversation with me that morning? Had God opened Phillip's eyes to the truth? For many such questions, I would never know the answers. Yet I know that Phillip had the opportunity to believe God's truth and to become a child of God that morning because God had urged me to paint a cross for Anna. I had not come to live in the village with the idea of painting crosses.

In this book, I ask the reader to take a trip with me. The trip will take us through phases of my life (childhood, college education, and missionary work in South America) as well as phases of my spiritual life and growth.

I hope that the experiences and thoughts in my striving to understand God's design for my life may also bring you to a better understanding of God's design for your life and the rewards of your surrender to His will.

TWO

FIRST THINGS FIRST

Therefore go and make disciples
of all nations...
teaching them to obey everything
I have commanded you...

—MATTHEW 28:19–20

God has a plan for your life, but it may not look like *your* plan.

Full surrender to the Creator of our souls is needed to allow Him to complete the plan He has for us. He is the author of this story, the potter of this vessel. My hope is not to glorify myself but to let His message shine through this story of my life. The artistic metaphors throughout the book are meant to illustrate our role as God's artwork.

Before I begin this story, I need to stop. Before I look backward or forward, I need to look up. This book is based on the reality of who God is. I believe a clear understanding of God is needed to bring relevance to this story. What is the nature of the God I surrender to? Who is the God who has a plan for my life and yours?

God is the Creator and sustainer of the universe. God is omniscient (infinite knowledge), omnipotent (unlimited power), and omnipresent (present everywhere). God exists realistically and independently of human thought. God is infinite and immensely larger than we will ever be able to understand.

God is self-existent, eternal, almighty, majestic, just, merciful, all-hearing, and strong. He is the Rock, our Father, Lord, and Master. He is able to strengthen us. He is our treasure, restorer, defender, helper, healer, highest ruler, and king. He will appoint, bring, call, change, determine, uphold, lay down, give, and take away. He is to be worshiped and served.

God is our maker and the author of our story, in which Jesus is the hero. He is intimately involved in our lives. We need to always remember that the world does not need us; we need God. We need a bigger view of Him and a smaller view of ourselves.

Humankind was cursed by the Fall. After the creation of the world, Adam and Eve decided they knew better than God what was best for their lives. They chose to not trust and obey Him, listening instead to the sly serpent that convinced them to question God. The principal job of the serpent—our enemy, the devil—is to deceive us.

We became separated from God after the Fall, and our focus fell from God to ourselves. When we hear God calling us back, we come as the Holy Spirit empowers us, redeemed by Jesus Christ for His glory. With our minds set on that thought, the focus is correctly shifted from ourselves back to Him. When we realize that we have no significance other than Christ in us, we begin to sense the urgency to show the world this same beautiful redemption. People without God are lost. He wants them found.

In Matthew 28:18–20, Jesus gives parting words to the disciples. Known as the Great Commission, it is a charge to all believers who are followers of Jesus. "Then Jesus came and said to them, 'All authority in heaven and on earth has been given to me. Therefore go and make disciples of all nations, baptizing them in the name of the Father and of the Son and of the Holy Spirit, and teaching them to obey everything I have commanded you. And surely I am with you always, to the end of the age.'"

If God has called you to Himself and cleansed you from your sins through the redeeming sacrifice of Jesus's blood and the Holy Spirit indwells your life, you are a follower of Jesus Christ. You are called to share His truths with those you know, those of your country, and those of far-off countries. Every believer is called to share the Gospel. Jesus is our example of humility and wild surrender to God. He taught the truth and loved people until it hurt.

The Holy Spirit enables us to go and be witnesses. In the book of Acts, Luke imparts Jesus's words to the other disciples. Acts 1:8 says, "But you will receive power when the Holy Spirit comes on you; and you will be my witnesses in Jerusalem, and in all Judea and Samaria, and to the ends of the earth."

Do you see who God is? Will you go
and show others God's great love?
Will you let God use you without desiring to steal
the glory?
We need to reflect God and not ourselves.

God, enlarge my view of you. Forgive me for being self-centered. Forgive me for trying to steal your glory. This life is about you, not about me. Without you, I am completely insignificant and empty. Open up my eyes wider. Help me bow lower. Shape me as I let go.

THREE

TRAILER PARK DIARIES

*Now we see but a poor reflection
as in a mirror...*

—1 CORINTHIANS 13:12

Early in my childhood, I knew what my weaknesses were. Coming from a broken home, we struggled financially, and I struggled in school. In thinking about identity, I did not want to be identified by my weaknesses.

While spending a week at summer camp when I was eleven years old, I felt God calling me to give my whole life to Him. I knew He was calling me to be a missionary in my public school and—in the future—in the jungles of some far-off country.

As a teenager, I was embarrassed to live in a trailer park. The connotation that comes with trailer parks was something with which I did not want to be associated.

Though I lived there, it was *not* my identity. My friends were those girls who seemed to have everything. They lived in big houses. They were smart, athletic, and musical, but they didn't share my faith.

In high school, I attempted to be involved in many things, particularly excelling in the arts, but my identity came from my faith in Christ. I wore T-shirts with Christian messages to school, led Bible studies, and never went to the parties I would hear about at the lunch table. I went to church a few times a week. I liked having people at school and church think I was holy. But I was not holy. I had hidden sin. I struggled with lust that took many years to acknowledge. I fought alone to overcome my weakness, always failing. I was not surrendered. My pride was the root of anything I did. I was doing the Christian life the way I thought it should be done, for all to see.

At the beginning of my senior year, I began attending a Christian school after attending the same public school for all my previous years. That was the start of a refining, humbling process. I had found my identity in being a Christian. It had always been clear-cut to me: either you were obviously a Christian, or you weren't. When I began to attend the Christian school, I assumed that everyone who attended was a believer in Jesus Christ. Then I began to see every shade of gray. The issue was no longer black and white for me. And so began a process of purifying what was on the inside of me as much as what was on the outside.

This process of transparency and sanctification carried into college and into today. Wild surrender is a daily choice; it is a chosen identity. How will I be identified? Will I be identified by weakness, by strength, or by my surrender?

God, you know my weakness. You know where I have been. You know all the things I have tried to hide. Help me put it all out on the table, hidden no longer. Thank you for the strengths you have given me. Lord, you put this song in my heart. You painted this soul with vivid colors. You knit me together with golden thread. Help me put these colors I love and the golden threads I hold tightly on the table. The beauty and the ashes I lift up to you. Do with it all as you have planned.

FOUR

ONSTAGE WITH REAL PEOPLE,
OR "THE PERFECT CYCLE"

For you created my inmost being; you
knit me together in my mother's womb.
I praise you because I am fearfully
and wonderfully made...All the days
ordained for me were written in your
book before one of them came to be.

—PSALM 139:13, 14, 16

When I was in high school, I enjoyed acting, sing-
ing, and dancing in our school musicals. The aim
was to perfect a performance that our audience would
enjoy. However, all those involved in the production
knew where the *real* drama was. It was backstage, in the
midst of logistical problems, personality conflicts, and
missing props.

11

Actors onstage and in movies have many admirers. A similar admiration is often directed toward people who are in full-time ministry. Pastors, worship leaders, and missionaries seem to have it all together. However, those onstage may be struggling with unseen issues. When I see people in full-time ministry, I assume they are perfect in every area of their lives. They seem to have neither weaknesses nor insecurities. I imagine that their lives must be better than mine. Automatically I believe they must have more spiritual discipline than I do. Their family members, I tend to assume, must also be perfect. I believe all these things until I get to know them.

If we view those in full-time ministry as perfect, knowing we ourselves are not, we may feel unworthy to be involved in ministry. Some people in ministry may intentionally attempt to appear perfect, hiding their weaknesses, so the cycle continues. The devil will try to use this misconception to keep future pastors and missionaries from serving. Or they may try to serve God in their own strength, hiding their weaknesses and sin. Then they are blindsided by the power that sin has over them, and their ministry falls apart as they fall deeper into sin. Transparency and accountability break "the 'perfect' cycle."

In ministry, when you are transparent both onstage and off, others will identify with you. When you admit that Christ is your strength in spite of your weaknesses, other believers will see that as they are filled with the Holy Spirit, they can be completely surrendered and useful in God's hands.

Some people I met over the years during which I was in full-time ministry assumed some very nice but untrue things about me. North Americans as well as Bolivians have asked me if my parents are missionaries or are also in full-time ministry. "No," I say with a smile.

My parents were each raised in average middle-class churchgoing families from two different North American states. Within both families, academic success was applauded, and high aspirations for the future were encouraged.

One evening while I visited my dad a few years ago, he handed me an old picture album. It was fun to see pictures of myself as a three-year-old with curly blond hair and a pink dress. I am the same person as I was in those old pictures, and yet I am so different now. I also saw pictures of my parents after they met in college. My mother had long blond hair and a countenance full of hope for the future. My father was tall with dark, curly hair. He was from New York and was different from anyone she had ever met in all of her eighteen years living on a small farm. My parents got married soon after they both graduated from college. They looked happy in all the photos, but I knew that was not the case.

My parents divorced when I was a child for reasons I will never completely know or understand. I felt that their divorce reflected negatively on me. It created a lifestyle different from those of my friends whose parents were married. I lived with my mom and older brother most of the time. My brother and I visited my dad on weekends.

My dad brought my brother and me to churches and Bible camp. He brought us to a Baptist church regularly on the weekends when I was six years old. One evening as I heard the pastor's words, I felt the Holy Spirit urging me to become a Christian. I walked forward to the altar to receive Jesus into my heart. The pastor's wife took me aside and explained salvation through the colors of the wordless book. God saved my soul, but He did not salvage my parents' marriage. Was heartache part of God's master plan for me?

Here I am, a product of my parents, whose lives are unique stories with some dark chapters. Being born into brokenness is part of who I am. I do not have to hide my parents' story and be ashamed. It is their story, a basis for mine, but I have a new story. I am a child of the King.

If you were to hear me give a Sunday message or sing a solo in church, you might mistakenly think that my life is perfect and that I have it all together. Well, there is no perfection here. My desire in sharing my family's history is to be transparent and vulnerable, so you can identify with me. Part of who we are is made up of our past. Our parents largely contribute to our early formation. My parents have stories of joy as well as pain and disappointment that make them who they are. We are all fallen, sinful people, but the scars of my past can weigh me down no longer. I will always be less than perfect, but

I am redeemed by the transforming power of Jesus Christ in my life.

You have a history that makes you who you are. God knows. He's been there through your joy and your pain. His plan is to use it all for His glory. Surrender your history into God's hands. You need not hide your stories in shame or hold on to them with bitterness. We've all made mistakes in our lack of obedience to Christ. Your past will never change. But as a fully redeemed person, your future in God's hands can have a powerful impact on those with similar scars as you live in victory and God gives you a *new* story. I challenge you to surrender everything and everyone from your past completely into Jesus's hands.

> *King Jesus, I surrender the people in my life into your hands. I give my family history to you. Help me be transparent with my life story and my pain. Direct my story. I want to obey you, be led by you, and glorify your name in everything I do! You can make all things beautiful. Jesus, you are the perfect redeemer.*

FIVE

JUNK COLLECTORS COME ON TUESDAYS

Come to me, all you who are weary and
burdened, and I will give you rest.

—MATTHEW 11:28

Tuesday is trash-collection day in the neighborhood where my mother lives. Garbage trucks come around on Tuesdays to pick up garbage, but those trucks will not take junk. Garbage and junk are different to them. Sometimes a man in an old, beat-up pickup truck comes along to take any left out metal objects, such as broken bicycles, old bed frames, or that exercise bike you never used. He knows where to recycle it to turn junk into money. Junk collectors want junk; they do not want garbage. No one wants your garbage. You have to pay to get rid of it.

It is easy to let broken or no-longer-useful things be pushed back into a corner of your basement, attic, or garage. They might have sentimental value or represent a lot of time spent. But there comes a time when we need to clean the house. We have to make the choice to get rid of the stuff we don't use anymore. It is clutter. It is extra baggage if we are ever going to move. There is no need to take it with us. Why keep broken junk? Get it out of the house.

Disappointments in our lives can be like big pieces of junk. They were once something promising and apparently good. Perhaps we put our time, effort, and hope into something that never turned out as we had planned. There is a watercolor painting on the wall at my father's house. I had painted it for a gallery art show when I was in college. I was proud of the painting yet never submitted it for the show due to a misunderstanding about the entry requirements. My heart broke as I walked through the crowded art gallery with not one of my paintings on the wall. The sadness that came from lack of recognition weighed heavily in my heart. What are we supposed to do with disappointments? When we hold on to them, they weigh us down. They cause heaviness in our hearts. We may rally after those heavy, downcast moments and look up with a new hope, but that disappointment is still there, pushed back to the dark recesses of our hearts.

We need to stop holding on to those disappointments. We need to get them out from where they have been stored and give them up. They are of no use to us now, and they are keeping us from moving forward. Holding on to disappointments can cripple us. Just as houses need cleaning, we need to take an inventory of our lives, getting rid of the junk. What unnecessary things are you holding on to? We need to consciously take our disappointments out of our hearts and put them on the curb for Jesus to take away. He can turn our worthless disappointments into something of value if we let Him. He desires for us to get the garbage out of our lives as well: the sinful habits that poison us. He will take that garbage and burn it up if we give it to Him. He waits for us to surrender our garbage and junk, so He can lighten our loads, freeing us to move where He wants us to go so we can do what He wants us to do.

> *Lord, you know the disappointments of my life. There have also been big plans and events that did not go as I thought they would. Like junk metal, their heavy memories are not useful. I need to give those up to you. I have disappointed myself and you. I have been let down by others. Help me take those things out from deep within and surrender them to you. That which I do not have the strength to give you, please take from me.*

SIX

Mess + Process = Perspective

*Because the Lord disciplines those he
loves, as a father the son he delights in.*

—Proverbs 3:12

On the wall of my favorite coffee shop is a painting of a baker making bread. With an understanding of the painting process, I realize that the artist must have begun with a base color of warm rust for the background. He or she would have painted the entire canvas first with one color before layering in the next colors. In the process of painting, it is only at the end that the painting comes together. In the creation stage, it may look like a *mess.*

When starting a painting, it may not even resemble what I hope the finished product will look like because it is necessary to lay a foundation, like a builder.

Foundations are necessary to build on top of, though they will eventually be partially covered. If you are not involved in the process, you see only the finished product, which is what an artist wants to show the world. The artist has no desire for the process to be seen, and in turn the world does not want to see the process; it wants to see only the finished product. We marvel at famous works of art that took great skill and time to finish. We look at the end product in a gallery or reproduced in a book. We see the result but know nothing about the effort in the creation.

Several people have commissioned me to paint pictures of their homes. Observers have commented on the completed paintings' appearances, but they have no idea of the process—how I struggled with the angles of the foundation of the house or repainted the building more than once. They do not know about the frustration with crooked windows or with colors that had changed many times before I settled on the final ones. Viewers do not know about the mess on the table where I worked. They did not see me working on the painting late at night. A vision of the finished product kept me working. I would never want someone for whom I was painting to see the mess of the process. That person might lose confidence in me, though I always have confidence in the process to create the desired result.

Likewise, the process of digging a hole for the foundation of a house creates disorder, but without it the house would not be stable. The architect who visits the building site knows the plans for his house. He walks through the construction site and sees materials piled everywhere with tools haphazardly strewn about and cigarette butts discarded on the ground. The house is under construction. Yet with joy, the architect imagines the finished product. His perspective is different from that of any other observer. He "sees" how the house will look when it is completed. To most people, the place looks like a mess, but that is a necessary part of the process that the architect understands.

God is intricately involved in the construction of our lives as He is building us up. He is not disgusted by the process or the disorder. He lovingly sees us as complete, even as He works on completing us. Like the architect of the house under construction, to God the house is beautiful because He made the plan and knows how it is going to look.

God's perspective is eternal. We can rest in His hands as He builds us. As we look around, we see others in various stages of completion. It is easy to be judgmental as we see the mess in their lives, but we are called to see others as God sees them: works in progress on the way to completion. Our heavenly Father has love and grace for us in our process. We need to extend that grace to others as well.

We are God's work of art. He is never finished with us. Sometimes we pull ourselves away from His protective care with our own decisions. When we come back to God, the architect of our lives, we will encounter discipline just as a child experiences discipline from a loving father. We need to surrender our limited perspective for an eternal one, allowing God to build our lives.

God, I see the mess in my life. I have set up idols in my heart, and I have dirtied this house. Help me surrender to your will. Build this building, Lord. Form this vessel so you are most glorified. Jesus, your redemptive work is beautiful. Though you see me as complete, I am not there yet, and you keep molding me into your likeness. Please continue to open my eyes to things unseen. Help me to trust you more. Give me an eternal perspective on my life and the lives of those around me.

SEVEN

THE POTTER VERSUS THE CLAY

Yet, O Lord, you are our Father. We are the
clay, and you are our potter;
we are all the work of your hand.

—ISAIAH **64:8**

The wind was frigid against my face as I trudged across the campus to the ceramics studio. Snow was quickly building up on the sidewalks. It was a winter evening during my junior year at college in Minnesota, and I needed to make a few more pots before the next day's ceramics review. Once I was inside the building, it took me a while to thaw from the freezing cold. Getting my tools and water out, I readied the table around my potter's wheel. Pulling out the heavy bag that contained the large block of solid clay, I cut off a chunk with my objective in mind: I would make bowls. Taking the clay to a large table, I slammed it down a few times to make it more round than square. Then it was ready for the wheel.

Art begins with the idea in the mind of the artist. He or she understands the media. The design will determine the creative process.

The will of an artist is the desire to bring the idea from his or her mind to a physical existence. The will provides the intrinsic motivation to start the process and to persevere until the artwork is completed. The artist is consumed with a desire to complete the work. Without the will, art is not made; it just remains in the artist's mind. I have known artists whose minds were full of ideas, but they lacked the will to follow through to see their ideas come to life.

The strength of an artist is in his or her ability, along with the tools, expertise, and material, to create the image that lives in her mind. A skilled and agile artist has all of these, as well as strength that does not falter. The work of his or her hands brings the design to life.

Our heavenly Father understands what each of us is made of, just as a potter understands the qualities of raw clay. The potter knows that clay is a type of dirt that comes from the ground. When clay is dug up, it has rocks, roots, and other matter throughout that were needed for its formation. Before it can be used to create pottery, the rocks and roots need to be removed. Then the clay needs to be refined even further. It is broken up into little pieces and dried. Finally, it is sifted through a screen so that no imperfections remain. As a fine powder, the clay is reconstituted with water and kneaded until it is workable.

Clay, though pure after the refining process, will always be messy to work with. The potter knows he will get dirty in the process. The potter takes the refined clay in his hands, and with much pressure he centers it on his wheel. The clay has to be pushed down hard onto the wheel in order for it to attach and spin together with the wheel. The potter needs to use water to let his hands slip over the clay's surface. The potter is in control, not the clay. As the ball of clay spins between his hands, he drives his thumbs down into the center, creating the inside space. Then, through a process of his hands working from the inside and out, he pushes and pulls the clay up into the form he desires to create. If a bump or imperfection is found, it could explode in the kiln, so it needs to be cut out; a delicate and very intentional process. As the pot rotates on the wheel, the potter takes a thin wire and, with both hands, gently slices off the imperfection. Some good goes out with the bad. The potter continues slowly pulling the clay up from the base of the pot with both hands mirroring each other inside and outside the pot, applying force to bring more height to the pot's walls. Since the potter understands the nature of the clay, he knows just how thin the walls are to be made before they are too thin and in danger of collapse.

God sometimes has to crush and rework us so that He will be glorified. In my life, heartache and disappointments have sometimes left me painfully bent out of shape. I can now look back and see that those times were the base for something beautiful. The Potter's hands were pushing down and nearly crushing me, completely reshaping the form this human pot was taking on.

When I was a senior in college, the day approached when I was to teach a class of junior-high students to satisfy an important requirement for my education major. The previous evening, I had dinner at a friend's apartment and stayed too long. I was not ready for teaching the following morning. I stayed up very late that night preparing, and in the morning I didn't wake up to my alarm. As a result, I overslept, missing the class I was to teach. I sped to the school to apologize, but the damage had been done. There was one very angry junior-high art teacher who did not have time for me to explain. Several days later, I gave the lesson, but the board of education of my college deemed that I had failed the experience due to my carelessness. They told me I would have to repeat all of my classroom obser-vations and pre–student teaching, thus graduating an entire semester later. It seemed a harsh punishment to me. I was crushed. I had failed. I had made a mistake and had to start over. At the time, it felt like the end of the world. I needed to learn better time management if I ever wanted to graduate!

It was a difficult period in my life, but from that crushing experience, I learned how to be more pro-fessional. During my subsequent attempts at student teaching, I was always prepared and on time. The co-operating teachers in the public schools had no idea how unorganized I had been prior to the unpleasant but necessary correction process.I needed that ordeal to shape me up.

After college, I searched for employment opportu-nities in a foreign country. I found and accepted a po-sition, teaching art at a Christian school in Santa Cruz, Bolivia. In addition to teaching art, I was assigned various other activities before and after the school day. I was also involved in my Bolivian church and helped at a local orphanage. Due to my hectic pace of commitments, I often did not eat a full meal for days at a time. My body was run down because I didn't let myself rest. I was broadsided by rheumatic fever, which stopped me from all activity. I could not get out of bed. I felt like I had arthritis in every joint of my body. With medicine and time, I rallied, but that crushing episode helped me realize I needed remolding—again!

God urged Jeremiah to go down to the potter's house. There, He spoke to Jeremiah and showed him that God Himself is the Potter, and His people are the clay. The potter is in control of the pot he is making; he has a plan for it. Then God showed Jeremiah that His rebellious people were like pots who looked up at their Creator from the potter's wheel and questioned their Creator about why He had made them like He did, questioning the work of His hands (Jer. 18:1–6; Rom. 9:20–21).

If you want to be moldable in God's hands, your mind, will, and strength have to be fully surrendered to the Master Potter. He is able to mold you (His clay) into a vessel He can use. Know your identity as the clay: your weaknesses, your strengths, your old and new natures, and the temptations that may never change. Fill your mind with scripture, and do what God is asking you to do. He has a plan for your life—the will to carry it out, and the strength to complete it. You are never beyond the Potter's redemptive hands. Allow Him to shape you into the image of Jesus Christ. He has proven Himself over and over. Trust Him.

Father, you are my Creator. Cleanse my mind as I spend time reading your Word. Speak to me in prayer, visions, and the words of the wise. You understand what I am made of. Put pressure on me; press me hard to form me into the vessel you want me to be. Cut out all the rocks and roots. Help me not try to control my own life but constantly give it up to you.

EIGHT

CROSS-CULTURAL LIVING

*May I never boast except in the cross of our
Lord Jesus Christ,
through which the world has been crucified
to me, and I to the world.*

—GALATIANS 6:14

I lived in Santa Cruz, Bolivia, for five years as the art teacher at an American Christian school. The school was a ministry to children of missionaries from several countries as well as to Bolivian students. Classes were taught in English. The school was like a little North American bubble. I was an authority in that setting.

Outside of the school, I was a student of the culture. It was my first experience living outside of the United States. I spent a lot of time with my landlord, her family, and people from the local church I attended. Not only did I learn Spanish from my Bolivian friends, but I learned customs and cultural norms too. My desire was to become part of this wonderfully different world around me. Before I could speak Spanish, my only option was to observe. I remember quietly going to church, listening, attempting to understand, and walking back to my house without having understood anything. I referred to my landlord as my Bolivian mother, and I was her *gringa* (white foreigner) daughter. Her family was my Bolivian family. I would sit with them in the circle of chairs in front of their house, sometimes right on the sidewalk. They would talk and laugh. I would listen and watch them. In time, I began to understand their jokes and laugh along with them.

In my first and second years in their country, I understood very little Spanish. Some of the girls and women with whom I became acquainted would pour their hearts out to me. After I began to understand their language, I tried to see their points of view. Some issues are the same in every culture; some are not.

My time living with a Bolivian family was great. My second-floor apartment consisted of a bedroom, a living room, and a bathroom. When I was in the house, I ate with my "family" in their kitchen. I usually left the house early in the morning to go to school, taught all day, and attended various activities in the afternoon and evening. I often returned to the house late in the evening, visiting with my "family" for only a few minutes. On the weekends and holidays, I saw more of them. Through five years, having lived in Santa Cruz with that dear family and a lot of time spent at my church and at church events, I thought I understood the Bolivian culture and people.

Several years into my time in Bolivia, there was a lot of political turmoil in the country, with strikes and protests on a regular basis. Bolivia was not a safe place, and American organizations were leaving the country. Our organization thought it best to have fewer missionaries on the field, considering that there were rumors of civil war. Two days later, I was on a plane to Peru with another single missionary woman who was also being evacuated by our mission. That month in Peru was like living in a different world. My eyes were opened to jungle living and ministry in an Amazon town.

After I'd spent a month in Peru, returning to Santa Cruz was a rude awakening. I was not sure that I was ready to be back in a city. I had enjoyed rural life and ministry!

I felt God reminding me of the desire I'd had long ago as an eleven-year-old child—to bring the Gospel of Jesus Christ to a remote area or village where there were no churches or missionaries.

Soon after that, I had an opportunity to visit just such a place. The pilot of my mission organization had occasionally flown pastors to the small village of San Fernando in eastern Bolivia to encourage, disciple, and evangelize. (There were few believers and no pastors or missionaries.) I accompanied the pilot and some missionaries on one of these flights. Upon meeting the few believers in the village, I learned that they desired to have someone come and establish a long-term ministry in the village.

We had dinner with the gracious leader of the church, a widow, and then walked around the grassy roads in the village, getting the official tour. Two little girls were my guides down to the river on that sweltering day. After they showed me the river, I spent time looking at a large, tin-roofed open structure that had dirt floors and no walls. It was the evangelical church where I would subsequently live and work. It was my dream come true to be a village missionary.

Later, we stood in the field that doubled as a landing strip, preparing to board the little airplane and return to the city. I needed to decide if I was going to accept the village's invitation. That commitment would mean no telephones, no Internet, and no daily contact with my friends. My only contact with civilization, as I knew it, would be through shortwave radio with the mission pilot and aviation mechanics back in the city of Santa Cruz.

The plan looked good to me. The list of ministry objectives was challenging: finish construction on the village's church and paint all of its adobe walls, plant a garden, get to know the families of the church and the leaders of the community, begin discipling those who wanted to grow in their walks with the Lord, become acquainted with the rest of the community, and build bridges for future ministry.

I was excited about working with a young woman who had a similar heart for ministry in a rural setting. She was a Bolivian around my age with extensive ministry experience. She was currently finishing seminary. However, as I prepared for the move, she changed her mind and decided not to move to San Fernando with me. A much younger girl named Reyna—a recent high-school graduate from a local church—was asked by her pastor to accompany me for the first six months until a more prepared woman could be found to be my ministry partner.

Newly settled in San Fernando, I believed I was ready to be effective in ministry. Added to my having lived in the country for several years, I'd received specific cross-cultural training.

Now I found myself talking to a wall, missing the mark with my young counterpart, Reyna. (The church building housed a two-bedroom apartment.) There I stood, deep in the jungle, speaking into the closed bedroom door, trying to communicate with Reyna, to no avail. She would not respond. We'd had a huge breakdown in communication. I tried to figure out what had gone wrong. Had I offended her? Was it a cultural issue? Did I cause her embarrassment in the community with my straightforward American ways? Was she tired of my poor Spanish? Was I forcing her to speak with me when she was not ready? Was it a lack of maturity on her part? Was I expecting too much from her? Was I expecting a depth she did not have?

When North Americans hear about my communication issue with Reyna, they want to know what the problem was, who was to blame, and how it should have been fixed. It is possible there was no problem with either Reyna or with me but simply a lack of understanding. Maybe we just had two different sets of worldviews/perspectives in life. Perhaps she valued what I did not, and I valued what she did not.

Life on the mission field often does not go as planned and sometimes turns out less than ideal. Flexibility is important. Plans change, people change, but God never changes. You always have to be looking for what you can learn from a situation. Just when you think you know something, you find there are more things you need to learn.

After two months in the village, Reyna and I returned to the city of Santa Cruz for a brief period. During that time, God healed our communication breakdown, and we were introduced to a Bolivian woman named Susan who would join our San Fernando ministry. Susan was around my age, and she had considerable ministry experience. She was currently finishing her seminary degree in theology, and she wanted to combine ministry in San Fernando with her thesis project. Susan lived and ministered alongside me in San Fernando intermittently for the next year and a half while she finished her thesis.

During the periods of time when Susan was not in San Fernando and Reyna had returned permanently to Santa Cruz, I had other companions to stay with me in the church. During one month, an older American woman joined me. For two months, Jane, a fifteen-year-old orphan girl from the village, stayed at the church with me. Jane did not seem to know how to talk to me. Sometimes she stared blankly at me when I asked her questions or asked her opinion. Rarely would she tell me what she was thinking. Over time, I realized that she would only tell me what I wanted to hear, or else she would not talk to me at all.

Jane did express interest in attending a boarding school for which I was willing to pay expenses. While she was staying in the church apartment, she seemed excited about the idea. We pursued the possibility. She and I journeyed to the city of Santa Cruz to stay for a few weeks and get Jane's personal-identification paperwork, which would be needed for application to the school. When we got back to the village and she was no longer living with me, I was mystified to hear through the grapevine that Jane did not want to go to the renowned boarding school at all. Did she change her mind but not want to tell me? Was someone changing her mind for her? Possibly she never wanted to go in the first place. We had studied Psalm 139 together. She heard how God had a plan for her life and that He loved her. Months later, when I heard about some of the activities she was involved with, I wondered whether she had taken to heart any of our conversations. Was it a question of cultural differences? I will probably never know the answer.

Subsequently, an older teenage girl stayed in the church apartment with me for a few months. She was from a neighboring community. Roxy had grown up in a loving, supportive home. She joked with me and asked me questions. She was a great companion. Roxy seemed to be confident in who she was and had no desire to rebel in any way. Neither of the teenage girls who stayed with me was able to help teach any of the Bible lessons or discipleship classes because they were not yet believers, but I appreciated their company. I shared God's love with them as we studied the Bible together. God knows their hearts. I pray His words penetrated deep into their souls.

We come into service for God with authority. Yet all too often we think we have authority to tell others we are right about so many other things aside from the Gospel. We only have a right to boast about the Gospel.

In San Fernando, God gave me authority to serve Him and to preach the Gospel of Jesus Christ. People came and listened to what I had to say. Throughout the week, however, I was in villagers' homes listening to and learning from them. The teacher must also be the student. We need to be teachable so that God can use us to minister cross-culturally.

Lord God, help me see the world through others' eyes. Help me in ministry to understand and appreciate things about others who are different from me. Forgive me for envying some and looking down on others, and help me learn from them all. I want to be teachable. Help me to not be stuck in my own way of thinking. Help me learn from others of different cultures. Help me step out of myself to have an eternal perspective. Lord, take this heart in your hands and mold it. Break it for what breaks yours. Use me to love people unconditionally.

NINE

THE GREEN-EYED MONSTER

Your hands made me and formed me;
give me understanding to learn your
commandments.

—PSALM 119:73

Susan spent a few months with me in San Fernando and then had to return to the city to finish her university course of studies. I was glad when she returned to the village once again to accompany me in the ministry. Susan was born in the mountain country of Bolivia. Her father was a country schoolteacher. She told me stories of her childhood in the mountains, a life very different from mine. Her family had moved a lot during her childhood, so she had gone to various schools. She started going to an evangelical church as a child and knew God's call on her life at an early age. By the time I met Susan in Santa Cruz, she had lived in four different states of Bolivia on her own as she served in various ministries and jobs and sought theological training. She is a happy person. If you met her, you would have no idea of the hardships Susan has lived through. She desires only to be used by God to bring people closer to Him. She and I come from very different backgrounds, yet we are very much the same in purpose. I praise God for Susan and for His perfect, creative plan to use every surrendered soul for His glory.

Even though I had blond hair and blue eyes and was a North American with a background seemingly very different from every Bolivian I had met, I loved living in San Fernando, teaching the Bible, and building friendships with the people of the small village. However, more than for teaching the Bible, I believe God brought me to the village to pave the way for others to come there and share the Gospel.

Susan had originally been allowed by her church to come to San Fernando only because I was already living there. Her supporting church had never sent a single woman out as a missionary to help another single missionary woman. I praise God that I was established in the village and that her church allowed her to come. She had a huge impact on the community. I enjoyed Susan's teaching too; it was biblically solid and captivating. On

Thursday evenings, when we went to a family's yard on the other side of the village for our weekly family Bible service, sometimes I did not teach. Children, women, youth, and a few men would gather. Often Susan would read an Old Testament Bible story, and it would come alive for all of us around the circle. She also had creative ideas for interactive teaching at the Saturday-night youth service—ideas I never would have thought of. When she led group games, everyone participated. She had a vibrant spirit, yet she needed her own space and time to be alone. Susan was serious about obeying God in all things. Beyond ministry and Bible teaching, she also took it upon herself to teach phonics to some illiterate boys. She was a skilled and patient teacher.

Being what we are—humans—there were times when Susan and I did not see eye to eye. We clashed on all sorts of things having to do with daily living, from cooking rice to feeding the chickens to washing clothes. One person's logic is not necessarily shared by another person raised in a different culture.

Susan and I were both strong-willed. The most divisive trick the devil used to consume and discourage us was the sin of envy. We envied each other. Envy stole our joy and unity. I envied Susan's ministries, which appeared to have more impact than mine.

My ministry became more inwardly peaceful when I remembered to find my significance in God. I stopped comparing myself to Susan. I began to enjoy teaching again, as I no longer felt she was judging me. God touched my heart and gave me freedom to sit and listen as she skillfully told Bible stories. I had accepted that I did not have the same reading and storytelling capabilities she did. I was learning to step back and appreciate her strengths, accepting my own weaknesses.

God—through His amazing grace—has shown me how to live surrendered in ministry. Humility must be held in the highest regard in everything we do. I've learned that I need to surrender control and trust others to lead. I've learned to not compare myself to others. It is crucial to encourage others' success and not seek personal recognition. We all need to remember that envy is a slow killer of ministry. Be sincerely glad that others are doing well! It is also healthy to let go of the controls and accept that others will be used by God the way He shows them, which might be different from the way He chooses to use you.

Thank you, God, for the ministries and contacts you have given me. Help me to be faithful to those people and to you. Help me to not envy others' ministries but to encourage them to be used by you.

TEN

A QUESTION OF PURPOSE

The Lord will fulfill his purpose for me; your
love, O Lord, endures forever—
Do not abandon the works of your hands.

— PSALM 138:8

One afternoon while living in San Fernando, I walked to my neighbor's house to have maté (a kind of tea). We chatted for a little while before two girls walked up to the house to do their homework with the woman's son. On the cover of one girl's book were pictures of world-renowned sculptures and structures: India's Taj Mahal, France's Eiffel Tower, and the United States' Statue of Liberty. Neither the girls nor my neighbor was familiar with the structures. I explained that the Statue of Liberty is a symbol of freedom, a beacon of hope. It is meant to inspire and welcome people. Immigrants from all over the world have come to the United States through New York City's harbor, welcomed by the statue. The huge sculpture is a silent leader. She blazes her torch for the world to see. Those who are able to see her in person or in a picture, those who desire freedom, and those who aspire to rise have looked up to her and have been inspired. How many of the advances of the United States were encouraged by the national sentiments of freedom, liberty, and justice reflected by the statue?

What is the purpose of art in society? Why do we make it? Why do we like it? Why do we need it? Why are there many different kinds of art?

Consider paintings: some are meant to transmit a sense of peace by showing a beautiful landscape. With soft colors and smooth strokes, the artist invites you to breathe and gives you permission to stop and rest.

There is a ten-foot-long mural painted across the sanctuary wall of Fuente de Luz, the evangelical church in San Fernando. The painting invites your gaze to bounce from lush green foliage populated with jungle animals and bright birds to a lazy river where a few alligators are relaxing, and then finally up to the brilliant colors of the sunset. The intention of the painting is to point to God, the Creator.

On the other hand, *Guernica* is a painting that sharply contrasts, in both purpose and appearance, with the river scene referenced above. Painted by Pablo Picasso in 1937, *Guernica* was created to promote an antiwar sentiment. This large work of art is full of dark, sad images of suffering and emptiness. It was created in response to the bombing of Guernica (a village in northern Spain) by German and Italian warplanes. The painting was commissioned to show the tragedy and suffering that war inflicts on innocent people.

The San Fernando river mural and Picasso's *Guernica* differ in purpose and appearance. Some paintings make you smile; others make you cry. Each piece of art has been intentionally created to have an impact on the viewer, whether it is to encourage, challenge, evoke desire or anger, or cause the viewer to remember days gone by.

God as Master Painter is intentional in painting *our* lives. He paints with the vision of the masterpieces we are to become. He desires to impact others through us if our lives are surrendered into His hands. Like a diamond with many facets and colors, each of us is unique, yet we are all to point to the same God. God paints us all into images He will use to show the world the truth of who He is and what He has done.

Potters make functional objects to be used for everyday purposes such as eating or drinking. A cup has a different shape from a plate, which reflects their differences in purpose. The design is meant not to make you think deeply but only to indicate the purpose of the object.

I took my first ceramics class when I was a college junior. There was a student in the class who was engaged to be married. He was determined to make plates, bowls, and cups as a wedding present for his fiancée. I didn't know the girl he was engaged to, but I can imagine that if she was expecting to receive dishes, she would be disappointed if her fiancé gave her a piece of art, such as a sculpture, instead.

Sculpture has a function, but it is very different from pottery. Sculptures are observed from a distance. Sculpture's purpose is to generate thought, inspire hope, or teach ideas. In general, sculpture is not meant to be touched and used like pottery.

Art's purposes vary from pottery, which can help deliver nourishment, to sculpture, which can inspire emotion. Similarly, there are a variety of purposes for our lives.

Like art on a wall or a sculpture in a park, God has made us to stand up and stand out. Our purpose is to cast vision, show truth, and lead people to the loving Redeemer. Some people do not see the need for art in society. I think they are similar to people who do not yet see their need for God's Word and His redeeming work in their lives.

Your Creator knows you. He has woven you together in a beautifully detailed fashion. He made your shape and your strengths, your weaknesses, and your personality type. You differ in appearance and giftedness from your sibling or your neighbor, but that's OK! God has a plan and purpose for *your* life. Understanding your unique purpose within the body of Christ will bring you satisfaction and contentment.

We need to listen to God and live in accordance with the way He made us. When we are surrendered into God's hands and let Him make us into the works of art He has planned us to be, we will glorify Him and benefit others. He has great plans for our lives, for His glory.

God, you have a plan and purpose for my life. I am made to seek you and let my light shine before men so that they glorify you. I am meant to be useful in your hands. Use me, Lord. Give me peace in knowing that there is a reason for everything that has happened in my life. Make a masterpiece out of my life so that people see you. God, have your way in me. Your will be done in my life.

ELEVEN

WHAT IS IT WORTH?

So is my word that goes out from my mouth:
It will not return to me empty,
but it will accomplish what I desire and
achieve the purpose for which I sent it.

—ISAIAH 55:11

One day I sat pondering the question: Was it worth spending thousands of dollars on a visual arts education and Bible degree at a private Christian college to then volunteer the next eight years of my life in South America? Some people might say that my time and money were poorly spent, and that those years were wasted since I have nothing tangible to show such as investments or a home of my own. The question of worth depends upon values.

My father saves things that others would throw away. He has some antiques that may be worth something to a collector. On the television shows that focus on antiques, people bring old things to professionals to find out how much they are worth. Some of the items are appraised for thousands of dollars.

There is a painting in my father's house that was done by my great-grandmother. The painting is a rendition of Dad's house in the woods. That painting may not be worth much to an art collector, but it is worth a lot to me.

Consider a simple line drawing of a face. If the drawing is an Henri Matisse sketch, it would be worth thousands of dollars according to professional art appraisers. The piece of art by Matisse has an internationally recognized worth. However, that same piece of art would not be considered valuable to my friends in a jungle village, who have a different perspective. They have a limited worldview and a simple economy. Few of them have graduated from high school, and most do not have electricity in their adobe homes. They do not value art, nor do they have the extra money to buy it. The villagers value animals, wood, and manual labor; those things have a fixed worth to them. Worth is relative.

While I lived in San Fernando, I painted some signs, a few murals around the village, and several crosses at the cemetery. I expected nothing more than gratitude in return. Someone in Bolivia asked me how much I would charge to paint a family portrait. I had to ask who wanted the painting. What I would charge to an American versus what I would charge to a Bolivian would be different. Painting was ministry in Bolivia. My village friends needed their money for buying food. When I did a painting in San Fernando for someone, they usually gave me things such as chicken eggs or fresh meat in return. The people of San Fernando were generous.

God used my life in Bolivia to show the love of Jesus Christ to many people. I had the privilege of sharing God's Word with them and the amazing honor of leading many people to a personal relationship with Jesus Christ. They were lost and now are found, were dead and now live, were slaves and now are free. How much is that freedom worth to you?

In God's economy, every human being has worth; so much so that Jesus was willing to pay for our eternal salvation with His life.

God, you are worthy. I bow to you and your plan for my life. It is worth it to give all I am to you. Fill me and use me to worship you now and every moment of my life. Help me not be concerned with my worth in anyone else's eyes but yours.

TWELVE

ISSUES OF THE HEART: THE UNTOLD STORIES

For the Lord searches every heart and
understands every motive
behind the thoughts
—1 CHRONICLES 28:9

As a single missionary in South America for most of eight years, I found that the most difficult challenges I faced were things you would never guess, and usually things I would never tell.

Homesickness was not what tore at my soul. Of course, I missed my family. I especially missed face-to-face conversations with my mom and my grandmother. I missed Caribou Coffee and Panera Bread. I missed certain conveniences. I missed the ability to explain myself, because I was not fluent in Spanish. It was a challenge to live in a different culture, but that was not the hardest part of my life as a single missionary.

While spending some time in the States after my first four years in Bolivia, in a moment of honesty with a group of ladies, I was asked what the hardest part had been. They were surprised to hear my answer: the most difficult thing had been having to say no to offers of flowers and chocolate.

Several times during my ministry, I met men who seemed to be placed by God in my path as possible life partners. There was a Bolivian youth pastor who worked at the school where I taught. During my first year of teaching, Matt caught my eye, and I know I caught his. We were both twenty-four years old. He was tall and handsome with a great smile and kind eyes. We spoke in passing. By the end of that school year, he wanted to call me and see me outside of school. I declined the offers because my mission organization frowned upon intercultural relationships during the first year in country. During my second year of teaching, Matt and I began talking on the phone and sending constant text messages outside of school. Midway through that school year, we had talked on the phone so much that our hearts were racing while we were dreaming about a future together.

However, during a time of solitude with God as I was supervising a junior-high-school retreat in the spring of that year, it became clear to me that Matt was not for me. I repeatedly tried to explain myself to him. Then when he still didn't seem to get the message, I felt I had to ignore him to show him I was serious. It was sad for both of us. Over the next months and years, he tried to give me chocolates and flowers to regain my favor, but God confirmed that this man was not for me. It was hard to stay strong as he tried so hard to win me back. Receiving flowers, chocolates, and jewelry does have a certain melting power over a girl.

Throughout the end of my fourth school year and into my fifth school year, another Bolivian man tried to steal my heart. He had heard me sing at a mutual friend's wedding. Months later, I met him at the same friend's birthday party. Daniel was outgoing and good-looking and was the pastor of a small church. He and our mutual friend invited me to sing at their church anniversary celebration. I accepted. The small church was still under construction on a dirt street in a poor neighborhood. Daniel invited me back the next weekend to see their Saturday-morning children's ministry. Both the ministry and his energy lured me in. Very soon afterward, I was going out to dinner with him and our mutual friends. Our friendship sped into a relationship, which got serious very quickly. After school let out in May, I spent lots of time with Daniel and his mother until I briefly left the city for a few weeks.

During those weeks away, I was on a trip with other North Americans up a tributary of the Amazon River to reach out to communities along the river. We traveled and lived on a barge for two weeks, sleeping in hammocks covered by mosquito nets. When I returned from that trip, I saw Daniel briefly for a few days, and we went shopping for an engagement ring like two crazy people. Then I flew to the United States to attend my brother's wedding. During that time in the States, through godly counsel with older women in the faith, God told me to slow down in my whirlwind relationship. I returned to Bolivia wanting to put physical space between me and Daniel so that we could continue to get to know each other spiritually and emotionally. Within two months, I had seen too many aspects of his personality that gave me doubts about a future together. I did not have peace from God to continue the relationship, so I broke up with Daniel. Soon after that, I spent a month in Peru (see chapter 8), which gave me time to distance myself emotionally from Daniel. When he called me sometime after I returned to Santa Cruz, while it was hard to not answer my phone, I knew that the relationship was not what God had for me.

In the spring of that year, a month after I came down with rheumatic fever (see chapter 7), I had an anaphylactic-shock reaction to a penicillin shot and nearly died on the floor of a small pharmacy's bathroom.

That was not my only shock of the month. Daniel had been accused of serious offenses, and his whereabouts were unknown. I was approached by his accusers to see if I knew where he was. These questions about his character confirmed that I'd made the right decision.

It is not easy for me to talk about issues of the heart. It makes me feel vulnerable and foolish. Being transparent shows my weakness as a single woman. Over the years, I have asked God to take these emotions away, even as I grew attracted to the kind, handsome American pilot who made occasional flights to the village of San Fernando while I served there. I have wished I could just worship God, serve Him in ministry, and not desire to be married. God never took my desire away. I began to fast and pray weekly for my husband—whoever he was, wherever he was. I also prayed that God would prepare me to be his wife. (A few years later, I met the right man; we were married in the United States and began a new life ministering in Houston, Texas. But that is a whole other story!)

In being transparent and letting you see my heart, I hope to break "the perfect cycle": trying to appear perfect. When we hide our weakness and sadness, we suffer alone and may fall into temptation.

As human beings, we are a combination of physical, spiritual, and emotional aspects. The physical and spiritual details of our lives are easier to talk about than the emotional details. It seems that the most difficult challenge of being a single missionary is the emotional aspect. The state of the heart paints everything. Our heart issues are unseen.

They are issues we are not expected to talk about or ask prayer for. In the past, I felt that issues of the heart needed to remain untold stories, that they must never be communicated to my co-workers or those who supported my ministry. The issues seemed too personal. I felt that talking about emotional issues portrayed me as too weak and thus unfit to be on the field as a single missionary, and that I needed to be strong. Well, yes and no: We cannot be our own strength. God needs to be our strength. We need to admit that we are weak by ourselves and need to let the body of Christ strengthen us.

I have incorrectly assumed that other single missionary women were stronger than I was, and that they did not struggle with issues of the heart like I did. I assumed very nice but untrue things about them. We are all real people with real heart issues. The temptation to believe that I am the only one with weakness is universal. It is also straight from the enemy of our souls to make us feel as if we are alone. He wants to divide and conquer.

Issues of the heart need to be addressed. Surrendering our emotions to God, being honest with ourselves, and being transparent to others are important. I look back and wonder why God put those men in my life. How much of those relationships were my fleshly desire for attention without listening to and obeying God? I had listened to relationship advice from other missionaries. When I finally sat still long enough to listen for God's voice, He said, "NO." I had not sought God's advice in my relationships. I hadn't sought God nearly enough before making phone calls or going places that invited harm into my life. My story could have been much different. It was only by God's grace that He kept me safe despite my bad choices.

God, who made our hearts, understands when they ache. I want to listen to His voice guiding me, but often I am too distracted by my own ideas. I need to identify and surrender the issues of my heart if I am to truly hear God and obey—to be willing clay, useful in His hands. He wants to use each of us to show His glory to the world. We will not fall to our fleshly desires if God is our strength.

Lord, I am weak and distracted. Strengthen me and help me be still. Holy Spirit, you know my anxious thoughts. Please do not let me step outside of your perfect will for my life, Father God. Help me be faithful today and not desire to be in a different season of life, wasting the one I am in. You are the author of all seasons. Let me live in a state of surrender to you today.

Be glorified in my surrender.

THIRTEEN

WHAT LISTENING LOOKS LIKE

Be still, and know that I am God...
—PSALM 46:10

Listening to God is a choice. Though God made us to have fellowship with Him, to listen and obey Him, our sinful nature screams, "Me first!" We are consumed with ourselves. We find it difficult to be still. We're like a box full of puppies, yipping and jumping and clamoring for attention.

While we were still in rebellion, God called out to us. He enabled us to hear Him. 2 Corinthians 5:17 says, "Therefore, if anyone is in Christ, he is a new creation; the old has gone, the new has come!" Even though we become new creations, we are still distracted. The devil will use anything to keep us from hearing and obeying our Master. When we stop and truly seek God, He will speak.

I shared Ecclesiastes 5:1–5 one evening in a San Fernando church service. In that passage, Solomon says that when we go near to God, we ought to listen rather than be in a hurry to speak. I gave the children paper and crayons. I asked them to draw what it looks like to listen to God. One drawing had a person with his hand up to his ear; another was of a person with huge ears. I gave paper and pencils to the youth and adults as well. Their assignment was to write a question to God, asking Him what He wanted to say to them and then to close their eyes and listen, and afterward to write the thoughts God had put in their heads. I picked up my guitar and began to play. The youth and adults wrote, and the kids drew. The church was busy, everyone in their seats writing or with heads down—eyes closed to pray and then eyes open to write. I wanted desperately to know what was going on in everyone's heads. I wanted the satisfaction of knowing what God was saying to them in that church service He had used me to lead. Out of pride and curiosity, I wanted to hear testimonies. But I didn't ask anyone to share. I knew that God was dealing individually with each one.

We need to learn how to listen. I asked the congregation to consider how much time we spend listening to God. Then I asked everyone to think about a person who talks constantly. I saw smiles on their faces and heads nodding in recognition. The talker has no idea of others' thoughts and needs. We often approach God as that talker. We are consumed with our own thoughts. We talk and talk to Him. God is patiently waiting to communicate with us, but we don't stop to listen.

In Jeremiah 29:13, God speaks through Jeremiah, saying, "You will seek me and find me when you seek me with all your heart." The truth implied by the opposite is that if we do not seek God with our whole hearts, we will not find Him.

When God is the authority in our lives and we are listening to His voice, the mandate is clear: reach out to all people of the world with His love. Our only response should be obedience.

In Psalm 139:23–24, David invites God to search him, to check to see what bad thing is still hidden within. When we ask God to reveal any wrong in us, the next step is to listen. We need to be sensitive to the leading of the Spirit but not be impulsive. As we approach the throne of the Almighty, we should not be quick to speak with many words but rather be still and disciplined enough so we can hear our Master's voice and obey. God will lead us to do what He made us to do.

God, quiet my anxious heart. I surrender my plans to you. Forgive me for acting like a puppy, jumping and making noise without listening to you. You are in control. I want to hear you. Give me self-control to be led by you. Help me be still.

FOURTEEN

BACK IN THE USA

*But rejoice that you participate in the
sufferings of Christ, so that you may be
overjoyed when his glory is revealed.*

— 1 PETER 4:13

Months after returning to the United States from South America, I sat alone in a café. A woman who I know walked in. As we started talking, she sat down. Then another woman came into the café to meet her. For the next hour and a half, I found out how much these ladies knew about knitting. After the knitting conversation, they discussed their children's lives. Then one of the ladies told us what television show she was going to watch when she got home. As they left, I could not help but be distracted by a conversation between two other women at a nearby table. They seemed to be in the jewelry business. After their business meeting, my heart went out to them as one spoke of her desire for real friends and the other about her concern for her rebellious daughter. After hearing about all these ladies' concerns, I wondered, *Where is God in their conversations and lives?* Those who do not have the Holy Spirit in their souls live in darkness; they are separated from God. They want wisdom, and they need light, yet they grapple in the darkness to get their bearings, trying to advise each other.

The woman who first sat with me at the café was a Christian, and she was a member of a group of women who knit together weekly. When she and I spoke several days later, I encouraged her to see herself as a missionary to her knitting circle, to use knitting as a means to reach these ladies for Christ. Our purpose as followers of Christ is to glorify God and worship Him forever in our conversations, jobs, pastime activities, and relationships.

A beloved former pastor of mine sometimes said, "For a few minutes, I'm going to stop preaching and go to meddling." And so I say to you, where is God in *your* conversations and in *your* life? Do you stop to think about your priorities and your purpose in life?

God has a plan for the lives of each of His children (Jer. 29:11). If we desire to follow Christ's example and teachings, our lives may move in a different direction than what we had planned or the directions our family and friends imagined for us. We need to decide if we will listen, obey God, and walk the narrow road that He has marked out for us, or if we will walk on the wide road that will lead to destruction (Matt. 7). Will you listen only to the voice of God?

As it often does, my mind travels back to South America. Here is the story of how one woman has walked that narrow road to follow Christ's example. She is known as Hermana Barbara in the village of San Fernando. She obeyed the voice of God to stand firm in her village and not leave despite devastation.

On a warm afternoon some years ago, young men were playing soccer in the center of the village. Two of the young men were Hermana Barbara's grown sons. One son from the city was visiting his family during his vacation. The other son was a teacher in the village school. A third son was sitting nearby with some ranch hands that had been drinking alcohol. A disagreement broke out. As Barbara's older sons left their soccer game to defend their younger brother, one ranch hand shot the two older brothers and then their father (Barbara's husband). In seconds, three men were dead, and the ranch hands got on their horses and rode away into the forest. The murderer was never caught.

I cannot imagine the depth of pain Hermana Barbara must have had in that moment and to this day. Yet she decided to stay in the village of San Fernando with her youngest son, who was not at the soccer field on that fateful day. Hermana Barbara could have moved to the city to be surrounded by more of her family instead of remaining in her primitive, isolated village with the constant reminder of the tragedy that took place there. But God has called her to forgive and stay, though the heartache doesn't go away. God has brought some healing to her wounded soul. She is the leader of the few believers in the village. She faithfully studies her Bible and seeks God to give her strength to be an example of forgiveness in that community, a village that has been sharply marked by many fatalities.

Hermana Barbara has impacted many lives—including mine—with her surrender to God despite heartache. She is a light in a dark place. She has learned to love like God, to have her heart break for the lost. She is consumed with the cause of Christ. You would never know her depth of pain by looking at her. She is completely humble and full of joy. Her entire existence is in service to others, always keeping God first as she lives for Him.

Despite advice from others and opportunities to live more comfortably in the city, she chooses to live as Christ, dying to herself every day in her village.

What are you doing that is of eternal significance? Where is God in your conversations, in your everyday interactions with others? Do you use your time wisely or waste it? How you use your time will show your true convictions. Do you value your comfort more than your impact on the world around you? These can be uncomfortable questions for believers. We can all learn from the example of Hermana Barbara.

> *God, am I willing to do whatever you call me to do? What is keeping me from doing your will? How do you want me to serve others? How can I live in a way that I will hear, "Well done, good and faithful servant" at the end of my life? Teach me to see through your eyes. I want to be moldable in your hands.*

FIFTEEN

FAITH IN A RECKLESS DESIGN

Now faith is being sure of what we hope
for and certain of what we do not see.

—HEBREWS 11:1

Often we Christians make good, safe plans without first consulting God. We may believe that in serving God and living by faith, we will do great things for Him, and He will give us victory. But if we surrender to God's seemingly reckless design for our lives, there may be physical risks and pain. In faith, we must fully trust that God is in control of the situation into which He asks us to step.

In Hebrews 11:23–35, we read about how Moses's parents trusted God fully as they hid him for three months and then put him in a basket and sent it floating down the river. Doesn't it strike you as a little crazy to put a baby in a basket in a river? But Moses's parents had faith that it was part of God's design. Many years later, God opened up a path of dry land through the middle of the Red Sea so that Moses could lead God's people to freedom. Think about the faith it took for all the Hebrews to walk that path! The passage continues to showcase prophets who, through faith, subdued kingdoms, obtained promises, stopped the mouths of lions, quenched the violence of fire, and escaped the edge of the sword. They all stepped out in faith, even though they didn't understand God's design.

Listening to God, surrendering our entire lives to His plan, and obeying fully will sometimes appear ridiculous to the world. Picture Peter in Matthew 14:24–29 stepping out of the boat onto the turbulent water as Jesus asked him to come. If there were other men in that boat who were not Jesus's disciples but were just along to help sail the boat, the whole scene would have looked incredibly reckless to them. Peter risked death as he took that step out onto the water to go toward what looked like a ghost!

Daniel 3:1–30 shows the audacious faith of three Hebrew boys who risked death to honor God rather than the king. King Nebuchadnezzar said in Daniel 3: 11, "Whoever does not fall down and worship, he should be thrown into the midst of a burning fiery furnace." Shadrach, Meshach, and Abednego would not bow. They responded to the king, "The God we serve is able to save us from it, and He will rescue us from your hand, O king. But even if he does not, we want you to know, O king, that we will not serve your gods or worship the image of gold you have set up." King Nebuchadnezzar was furious and had the three Hebrews thrown into the fire. Yet they were not burned as they walked out of the fire untouched. The three Hebrew boys were ready to die for the glory of God. They had faith that God would be with them as He delivered them straight to Heaven or as He protected them from the flames. They trusted that God was in control, not King Nebuchadnezzar. God must have been overjoyed to see His children trust Him as they lived out the perfect design He had for their lives. Wildly surrendering in obedience to God will look illogical to the world around us.

In Acts 6 and 7, was Stephen's faith any different from that of Peter or the three Hebrew boys? Stephen was filled with the Holy Spirit. He spoke God's truth to a volatile audience, and he was stoned to death. He took the risk, obeyed God, and died. That was God's perfect design for Stephen. Was it a waste of Stephen's life? Could he have kept his mouth shut and lived longer? Obeying God and following His perfect design for our lives may not make sense to us at times, and they come with real risk. There is a price for obedience.

There is a passage in Hebrews 11 where faithful people trusted God, and they were tortured with cruel mocking, scourging, and imprisonment. They were tempted, they were stoned, they were sawed in two, and they were slain with the sword. Are we willing to be that faithful? Are we willing to risk persecution and physical harm in obedience to the Lord?

We are foreigners in this world, travelers. Heaven is our home. God is our King, our Potter, a Father who loves us, and He is preparing a place for us in Heaven. We are called to a risky life of faith, bringing His truths to places where it may be awkward or dangerous. Are we willing to follow God's perfect, "reckless" plan for our lives? His will is that we surrender to Him all that has happened in our lives along with our strengths and our weaknesses and love Him with our whole being, allowing Him to transform us into Jesus's image.

God, I know there are risks in this life of obedience to your perfect plan for my life, but I trust you with my life. Be glorified and make your name famous on the earth through me. Prepare me and use me in the ministry you are calling me to. Help me take risks to live this life of faith.

SIXTEEN

WILD SURRENDER

If anyone would come after me,
he must deny himself
and take up his cross daily and follow me.

—LUKE 9:23

The words "wild" and "surrender" do not naturally fit together. What does "surrender" mean in comparison to "wild"? What do they mean together?

"Wild" can mean unconventional, uncivilized, living in a natural state, risky or imprudent, uncontrolled emotion, enthusiastic or lacking restraint, unpredictable, not tamed.

Wild animals act according to the instincts that God gave them. Without conditioning by man, wild animals do not act outside of their nature.

When I lived in the Bolivian jungle village, I often went jogging on the road heading south. Moments after starting my jog, I'd find myself surrounded by tall trees on both sides of the road with colorful birds gliding overhead. I usually went running in the early morning or the early evening. Occasionally I would hear a low, steady roar like the sound of a brush fire in the distance. My neighbors later told me that the distant roar was the *manechi* or howler monkeys.

I heard the *manechi* many times but saw them only once. I had been invited to a birthday lunch for a woman at a ranch near the *manechi* habitat. To arrive at the ranch, I walked forty-five minutes in the jungle along the river and then crossed the river in a dugout canoe. After lunch, the kind people of the ranch took me deep into the jungle to see the *manechi*. We reached a canopy of trees that was higher than any I had seen before. The *manechi* were not making a sound as they only howl at dawn and dusk. The monkeys were so far up in the trees that I could not make out much detail, but I could tell they were *big*...and *they were looking at us*. No one at that ranch or in the village had *manechi* as pets. They are truly wild and are meant to stay that way.

Who tells the *manechi* how to live high up in the canopy? Some people might think that the *manechi* act reckless as they jump from tree to tree, but they act in accordance with their nature. They have a strong tail that is often five

times their body length. The tail can be used to grip a tree and support their body's weight. The *manechi* have shell-like vocal chambers that enable them to be clearly heard up to three miles. They make more noise than any other animal as a means of defending their territory. They are not designed to be tamed by man or live in a cage. The *manechi* act according to God's perfect design.

There is a perfect design for each of our lives that calls for us to wildly surrender to the Creator of our souls, to be doing what God created each of us to do.

After having lived in the village of San Fernando for seven months, I was happy to receive a projector to show movies and Power Points for the church service. A generator supplemented the solar-powered electricity that was needed to run the projector. When the system was working like it should, it was wonderful. I showed some animal movies just for fun. We also watched movies that showed examples of people's transformed lives. But no movie is as powerful as the Jesus film. One scene that always catches me off guard is the scene of Jesus getting angry in the temple. He is enraged at all the vendors making money for themselves in God's house. Jesus seems reckless in His actions as He turns tables over, driving out the money changers and generally causing a huge ruckus. This scene is always shocking to me when I watch it, as I am sure it was for my village friends as well.

While watching Jesus talking with His disciples and healing people in the movie, I did not expect to see this wild behavior from Him. As far as we know, He did not go around to temples on a regular basis, flipping tables and letting the animals out of their cages. Yet if you understand God's heart about the issue of the misuse of His house, the event is completely within Jesus's nature.

Imagine, if you will, a disciple who was with Jesus one day. That disciple might have thought to himself, *Jesus was brought here to heal this little girl, but when we got here, she was dead. He's telling her to wake up. What's going to happen if she doesn't get up? That could be embarrassing.*

Jesus is totally committing here; it's all or nothing. If He can't do it, I'll pat him on the back and say, "Better luck next time, Jesus. You can't win 'em all."

Imagine yourself in that disciple's place as he might have described what happened next. "So, Jesus is still looking down at the little girl, and…*WHAT IS HAPPENING?!* I can't believe my eyes! The little girl's eyes opened! People gasp; some shriek. It is *unbelievable.* Jesus did it again! The little girl was *dead,* but now she is sitting up! She's even *eating* something. Now Jesus calmly turns to go; His purpose is done here. He glances back at me, my eyes still wide and my mouth hanging open. He has a grin on his face and says, 'Come on,' motioning that we leave the house. I follow him, just seeing the back of His head as a few people quickly crowd in front of me. I look around, seeing people crying with joy. Some are jumping and shouting, hugging each other with tears that have turned from sadness to joy. Other people are just as shocked as I am. I've seen Jesus do miracles before, but this one leaves me speechless."

That is our wild Jesus! He took what looked like risks: walking on water and telling the blind to open their eyes and the lame to walk. He lived the perfect reckless design for His life that God had planned for Him to live.

The dictionary definition of surrender is "*to relinquish possession or control of*" and "*to give up or abandon.*" When a believer surrenders, he or she gives up his or her own will and subjects his or her thoughts, ideas, and deeds to the will and teaching of God. Surrender in this case is a dying to self or emptying of self. It is a submissive behavior. Jesus's excellent example of surrender in Philippians 2:5–8 is humbling, to say the least. Jesus was God, and yet He made Himself nothing, taking on the nature of a servant. It made no sense to a people waiting for a Messiah King, who they were hoping would have grand prestige and ruling power. Those people could not imagine that the son of a carpenter could be their King. His life contradicted their expectations of a messiah, but Jesus was totally surrendered to God's design for His life. He was guided only by His Father's voice.

Wild surrender is Peter stepping out of the boat onto the water when Jesus calls to him in Matthew 14:28–29. Peter surrendered his logic, his will, and his thoughts as he obeyed Jesus. We remember that Peter looked down and doubted and began to sink. We shame Peter for doubting, but we need to applaud him for stepping out in the first place.

God calls us to surrender our plans and our man-made logic to follow Jesus. He may ask us to live in a way that looks reckless to the world around us.

Living in wild surrender to the Creator of our souls is not passive. To have a spirit-led life is neither mystical nor complicated. Accepting who God has made us to be, using the abilities God has given us, is where freedom is found. Ask God to lead. Listen to Him and obey. We need to move when He tells us to move and stop when He closes doors.

Listen constantly; never stop seeking His face. God loves you and desires to do great things through your life if you are willing clay in His hands.

> *Lord, lift my gaze and quiet my heart. I want a wild faith: the faith you made me to have, with a complete surrender to do whatever it is you want me to do. God, mold me into the vessel you can use to glorify you the most. Pull me deep into your word; I want to be consumed by you. God, I love you; I need you. Make me. Holy Spirit, inhabit me. Lead my steps. Have your way in me.*

SEVENTEEN

CHALLENGE TO NORTH AMERICAN YOUTH

LISTEN, youth from the United States: You have been born into an age of privilege, freedom, and opportunity. Look where you are in history. You have opportunities at your fingertips. Using the Internet, you can be connected with nearly anywhere in the world. There are opportunities to study, work, and travel like never before. The economy of the United States is strong. Gender equality is valued. Socioeconomic advancement is possible; growth and change are welcome.

Everyone is born into a system, a worldview, a set of norms. God chose you to be born in the United States of America for a reason. God is calling and enabling you to reach the world for His glory with your giftings. There are many mission organizations and ministries to be involved with. Now is the time for American youth to step up and decide to be useful in God's hands, not just take up space on earth as one more person looking for ways to make his or her own life comfortable.

You have a choice. Do you live in a privileged nation only to enjoy the comfortable life? Or is there something more? If you live only for yourself and ask God to bless your plans, how can you expect Him to use you? You may say, "God, use me for your glory," while you think, *If it is safe and if it will benefit me in the end.* Do you make empty promises, telling God you will do anything for Him but not really meaning it? With all the financial investing and concern about physical things and comfort, who is investing in eternity?

Queen Esther was born a Hebrew, but through a series of events orchestrated by God, she became queen, married to the king. When genocide was looming over her people, she had a choice. She could do nothing and continue to enjoy her lavish life in the palace, or she could trust God and take a risk in the hope of interceding for her dying people.

You are surrounded by privilege for such a time as this; there is a world hungering for the Gospel that you have the ability and mobility to impact for Christ. Without a saving faith in Jesus Christ, people are lost. They will never know about God if no one goes to tell them. God can work through you if you are willing. He wants your whole life. God can only use willing and moldable clay.

Are you willing to accept God's design for your life, even though it may look reckless to the world? Will you wildly surrender to your Creator?

You are called. You are chosen. God will enable you to step out of the boat!

EIGHTEEN

CHALLENGE TO THE NORTH AMERICAN CHURCH

I grew up in a typical, Bible-believing, moderately con-
servative North American church in upstate New York.
I lived many years of my life surrounded by followers of
Jesus Christ. I find it comforting to worship God together
with other believers. I enjoy going to church. It is always
exciting to go to a Christian conference or concert. I
imagine that many of you feel the same way.

Do we get just as excited about investing dollars and
time in reaching others for Christ?

I praise God for many North American believers who
gave faithfully to my mission so that I could live in Bolivia
and reach people with the love of Jesus.

North American Christians can have a powerful impact on world evangelism. I wonder if the devil smiles

when we put in our 10 percent and then fill our lives with activities like Bible study or church meetings, thinking we have done all that is required of us. We become focused on the Bible, but we rarely share it with anyone. Not sharing the Gospel with the lost is like letting them die as I look the other way. Do I value their lives? Do I invest in eternity?

I challenge you, the affluent North American church, to stop and look at your life—what you have and how you spend your money.

There is a way to multiply our influence and invest well in eternity. I would like to connect North American affluence with South American availability. Latin America has been receiving North American evangelical missionaries for over a century. Missionaries planted churches and opened seminaries that are now run by nationals.

There is a relatively new mission movement in Central and South America that is very exciting. There are many solid, mature, growing Bible-based churches and seminaries, even though Latin America is not completely evangelized. There are still villages with no evangelical witnesses and other towns that persecute evangelical Christians, yet in the last fifteen years, there has been a call to the nationals of Central and South America to prepare and be sent as missionaries within Latin America and to the world. I have seen Bolivians called to missions, trained, and sent as missionaries; young men and women are stepping up to share the Gospel in places where it is not presently preached. I was thrilled to have Susan minister alongside me for part of my two years in the village of San Fernando. Born in the western mountains of Bolivia, Susan received her theological training at a seminary in central Bolivia and was financially supported by her Bolivian church. When I left San Fernando in 2012, the village had its first full-time pastor. He and his family were sent as missionaries from the city of Santa Cruz, supported by national churches.

I have seen youth from South America reach deeper within their own countries and beyond. I have met Bolivian missionaries to India, Japan, Pakistan, Kenya, and two other countries I cannot name for security reasons. It is thrilling to see South American youth who desire to obey the Great Commission and go wherever God sends them. Latinos can be more effective than many North Americans in third-world mission fields and creative-access countries. As Christians, we may be color-blind, but the world is not. There are places where it would not be safe for a blond, blue-eyed woman to go. Hispanic culture, world view, and general physical appearance make them better candidates for world missions.

North American churches can have a large influence in mobilizing Hispanic missionaries. Latin youth are being called and prepared as cross-cultural missionaries, but in order to be sent, they need supporting churches. Latin churches are warming up to the idea of sending their own missionaries, but some churches, even though they understand their financial responsibilityto send missionaries, do not have the funds to do it. That is where every church needs to see itself as part of the body of Christ worldwide and work together to reach the rest of the world for Christ. Bolivia, for example, is the poorest country in South America. I believe the North American church can help make Latin American missions more possible. I love the idea of South American churches financially supporting their own missionaries, but sometimes it is just not possible.

You have a choice: Will you live your life so safely that you never step out of your boat and never join Jesus walking on the water? Or will you listen for God's voice, stand up, and take your part in the global church to reach the nations with the Gospel of Jesus Christ?

Will you ask God to show you His perfect yet possibly reckless-appearing design that He has for your life? Will you live in wild surrender to the Creator of your soul?

NINETEEN

CHALLENGE TO THE YOUTH OF CENTRAL AND SOUTH AMERICA

God is calling you! God has made you specifically for such a time as this to go and reach nations with the Gospel. There is an adventure with your name on it. There is a challenge only you can meet. There are lost people who need to be found. God has given the keys to you to unlock eternity's doors for those who are perishing.

A century ago, the United States and Europe headed the evangelical missions, sending missionaries all over the world to bring the Gospel of Jesus Christ. Many missionaries went to South America to reach lost people for Christ. Many have been saved by the power of the Holy Spirit. Churches, schools, and seminaries were born as a result of the foreign missionary effort. Some of you come from families that have been Christian for many generations, reaching back to the impact of the first missionaries' visits to your countries. South America, Central America, and Hispanics in the United States now have vibrant evangelical churches with mature believers who are growing in their faith. Some of you have reached into the poor neighborhoods of your city to show the poor and disenfranchised that God loves them. God has opened your eyes and hearts to reach those in your city who are caught in prostitution and drug abuse. Or maybe God has called you to reach the financially elite who are just as lost without Christ. Now lift your eyes up past your town and your country to the world!

It is your turn to go to the entire world, reaching every nation for Christ. Your eyes, your skin, your nationality, and your wild surrender to the King of Kings qualify you to be a cross-cultural international worker who brings light into the darkness. You are perfectly fitted to go into countries where many Caucasian North Americans cannot. Will you be faithful and go? Will you stand with the global church and be the soldiers on the front lines? Will you be consumed by the call of Jesus Christ? Will you let the Holy Spirit be your shield and your strength? Will you be Jesus's mouth, hands, and feet in the nations? Are you willing clay in the Potter's hands? What are you holding on to that keeps you from the call of Christ?

We need the maturity that comes with solid Bible training and a readiness that comes from a willingness to die. There is an army that has been building—a revolution is coming! You have lifted your hands in surrender to God, your Father. You love Him, and you want to live for Him, but are you willing to go? Will you give your whole life to reach the lost? Will you accept the challenge that Jesus gave to go to the entire world with His message of Salvation?

God has a very specific plan for your life in world missions. God knew the plan for your life before you breathed your first breath. He designed you to hear His voice, be moldable in His hands, and live a life of obedience that may appear reckless to the world. He is calling you to have a reckless faith in your wild surrender. He has called you to be part of His revolution for Christ in this lost world. God has called *you*. All you need to do is step out of the boat like Peter. Every day you will need to surrender your will to God—the Artist of your soul. You may be afraid as you step out of your boat of security, but look straight into the eyes of King Jesus. He will give you strength and direction, and He will be glorified as a result of your trust in Him.

Will you stay in your churches, where it is safe? Will you keep your faith to yourself? God is able to supply all your needs according to His riches in glory. Surrender and expect to be amazed, South American and Central American youth!

Go to all the world. You are called. You are unique. You are chosen. You are loved.

By God's grace, you are able.

Step out of the boat!

TWENTY

CHALLENGE TO THE LATIN CHURCH

Brothers and sisters in the faith of South America and Central America! God is preparing you. He has called you to Himself in His wonderful grace for a reason. God wants to be glorified. He has redeemed you to show His power. He has forgiven you to show His amazing grace. God continues to show you new things in His Word because He loves you. Now He wants your faithfulness, your complete surrender. God wants your maturity. He wants you to grow in your faith and hear all His words. He wants you to obey Him completely. You know the command of our Lord Jesus from Matthew 28:19–20. You have been faithful to invite your neighbors to church. Now the call goes further. God is calling you to reach all towns, countries, and nations for Him. You are able with God, who is your strength. Hear the call to be involved in something so much bigger than yourselves. Be part of Jesus's Great Commission!

You have been faithful in teaching your children in the ways they should go to serve the Lord. You have led by example in your churches. God has enabled you to serve Him in full-time ministry, to give sacrificially to those He has called to be in full-time ministry.

Now I believe that God is calling youth in your churches and cities to obey His call to go to the entire world.

In order for me to have served as a missionary in South America, many believers in the United States financially supported me for the entire eight years. Without them, there would have been no way for me to go to South America. I am grateful to all of those faithful believers who took seriously the call to support the Great Commission of Jesus Christ. When I was with my supporting churches in the United States, I often showed them pictures of my ministry in South America and explained what their involvement meant to me and to many people in South America whom they would never meet. Many North Americans saw my ministry presentation, but only a core group of believers were the faithful ones to financially support me for the entire eight years.

Will you be faithful with your finances? Will you be faithful with your time and the resources God has entrusted to you? God sees your heart. He wants your willing surrender. Encourage the youth around you to listen to God's calling to go. You can teach and support them.

Or perhaps God is calling you and your entire family to step out in reckless faith and go to the nations. You have three choices: give, go, or disobey. Understand your role in the body of Christ, His church. The body has a mouth, eyes, ears, hands, and feet. God is the heart, Christ is the mind, the Holy Spirit is the air breathed by the body, the youth are hands/feet/mouths, and you are the muscles. *You are needed* for the body of Christ to be effective. You can be a strong support. You are called to action.

> Will you listen for God's voice? Will you be obedient
> in what He is asking you to do? Are you moldable?
> Are you the clay that God can use?

I believe God is calling Hispanics from all over the globe to reach the rest of the world for Christ. "Dios está llamando a los Latinos. Es tiempo de despertar! Si ya eres Salvo, ahora debes alcanzar a otros; el mundo está muriendo sin Cristo! Fuiste salvado para cumplir un propósito, ahora. Esta libro no es solo para entrenerte, intenta encenderte!"

To the Reader

Learn how to become an international worker or support the work of Hispanic international workers who want to obey the Great Commission but who do not have the funds to go to the ends of the earth.

For more information, contact Dana Wilson, International Missions Representative with South America Mission for nearly twenty years—living in Bolivia—and director of the ministry PROCLAMA, which prepares Hispanics for international missions work and prepares churches that want to be more involved.

Dana Wilson
dwilson@southamericamission.org

Teach in South America with South America Mission. Give a year or the rest of your life!

Contact Sue Post
SAM development
spost@southamericamission.org

Contact for any questions.

Katie Wells
International worker, author, speaker, and artist
kwells@samlink.org

Made in the USA
Monee, IL
11 May 2020

30697586R00059